How DeepSeek's Janus Pro Works

The Cutting-Edge AI Model Transforming Innovation

Owen Delaney

Copyright

Disclaimer

This book is intended for informational and educational purposes only. While every effort has been made to ensure the accuracy and completeness of the information provided, the author and publisher make no warranties, express or implied, regarding the content's reliability, timeliness, or applicability to any specific situation.

The views and opinions expressed in this book are those of the author and do not necessarily reflect those of any organizations, companies, or individuals mentioned. This book does not constitute professional, legal, financial, or technical advice. Readers are encouraged to conduct their own research and consult with qualified experts before making any decisions based on the information provided.

Additionally, references to companies, technologies, and individuals are for illustrative purposes only and do not imply endorsement or affiliation. The author and publisher disclaim any liability for any direct, indirect, incidental, or consequential damages arising from the use of this book.

Table Of Contents

Introduction

For years, the artificial intelligence industry has been dominated by a select few—tech giants with seemingly limitless resources, billion-dollar research labs, and proprietary models that dictate how the world interacts with AI. They've built astonishing systems, pushing the boundaries of machine learning and automation. But for all the breakthroughs, one thing has remained constant: access to cutting-edge AI has always been controlled.

Then something changed.

A new player emerged—not from Silicon Valley, not from a trillion-dollar corporation, but from a team with a different vision. Their mission wasn't just to compete with AI giants—it was to change the game entirely.

That player was DeepSeek, and their creation, Janus Pro, sent shockwaves through the industry.

With a development cost that was a fraction of what industry leaders were spending, Janus Pro delivered results that rivaled the best. It wasn't just powerful—it was efficient. It wasn't just impressive—it was open. And most importantly, it proved that AI innovation didn't have to be monopolized by a handful of companies.

Suddenly, the old narrative was shifting.

AI development, once thought to be reserved for only the most well-funded tech companies, was now within reach of a much broader audience. Researchers, developers, and businesses that had long relied on the tools of Big Tech now had something new to consider—an alternative that challenged the notion that advanced AI should be locked behind corporate walls.

This book takes you inside that shift.

It unpacks the technology behind Janus Pro, explores what makes it different, and examines its implications for the future of AI. More than that, it asks a fundamental question:

What happens when the biggest names in AI are no longer the only ones leading the charge?

As you read, you'll gain a deeper understanding of:

How Janus Pro works and why it's turning heads in the AI industry

Why efficiency and accessibility in AI development matter more than ever

What this means for the future of artificial intelligence, innovation, and competition

This is not just a book about a model.

This is the story of a changing landscape—one where AI is no longer just a tool for the elite, but something more open, more powerful, and more disruptive than ever before.

A new era of artificial intelligence has begun.

Turn the page, and step into the future.

:

Chapter 1

The AI Landscape Before Janus Pro

Before Janus Pro emerged as a groundbreaking force in the world of AI, the landscape was dominated by a small group of tech giants who set the rules, shaped the direction of innovation, and controlled the future of artificial intelligence. OpenAI, Nvidia, and other established players in the tech industry had the resources, the talent, and the data to build powerful models that revolutionized various sectors. But while their models dazzled with capabilities and unprecedented performance, there was an underlying issue—their very dominance created a bottleneck. Access to their powerful systems was limited, and the cost of developing similar models was far beyond the reach of most smaller players in the market.

In the early days of AI, companies like OpenAI and Nvidia were the undisputed leaders. These companies had mastered the art of building highly sophisticated deep learning models, using vast amounts of data to train their systems. Their success led to the rise of impressive applications: from language models like GPT-3 and GPT-4, capable of generating human-like text, to image-generating tools that could produce artwork based on text prompts. AI was no longer a theoretical concept but an essential part of the technological fabric that underpinned major industries—from healthcare and finance to entertainment and beyond.

But as these companies made waves with their innovations, a problem began to surface. The gap between AI's potential and its accessibility began to widen. While the technology was available to a select few, the average researcher or smaller startup was locked out. OpenAI's GPT models, for example, were incredibly powerful but also incredibly expensive to access, with limitations on usage for those who couldn't afford the hefty fees.

Similarly, Nvidia's GPUs, the hardware driving much of the AI revolution, were vital for training models, but their high costs and scarcity left many smaller companies scrambling to catch up.

This created a paradox. While AI had the potential to change the world, it was simultaneously concentrated in the hands of a few players, leaving smaller innovators, independent developers, and emerging companies on the sidelines. At the same time, there was an undeniable demand for a more efficient, affordable, and open-source approach to AI development.

AI enthusiasts and technologists were clamoring for something that would level the playing field—something that didn't require massive budgets to develop or deploy. Researchers, coders, and entrepreneurs wanted access to powerful AI systems that could be fine-tuned for specific tasks, applied to unique problems, and experimented with freely. The costs and barriers to entry were creating a bottleneck in the rapid expansion of AI technologies. Innovation was stifled not by the lack of ideas or talent, but by the resources required to build and access these tools.

As the demand for more efficient AI grew louder, the AI market began to feel the pressure to evolve. The traditional approach, in which a few tech giants controlled the landscape, seemed outdated. There was a clear need for new solutions—something that could deliver high performance while also being affordable, open-source, and available to a wider audience.

This is where DeepSeek's Janus Pro came in, offering a stark contrast to the existing models that dominated the field. But before diving into the revolutionary aspects of Janus Pro, it's important to understand the state of the AI landscape and how it led to the creation of such a disruptive innovation.

The Dominance of OpenAI, Nvidia, and Big Tech

For much of the past decade, OpenAI and Nvidia held a near-monopoly over the AI landscape. Their influence was undeniable, shaping not only the development of AI models but also the infrastructure needed to support them. OpenAI's GPT series revolutionized natural language processing, while Nvidia's GPUs became the essential hardware for deep learning. These companies had the financial backing and expertise to push the boundaries of what AI could do, setting new standards for innovation.

But with this power came a tremendous amount of control, creating an ecosystem where only the wealthiest players could thrive. As powerful as their models were, the question remained: How could smaller companies and independent developers tap into this potential without the exorbitant costs associated with using these tools? Janus Pro emerged as an answer to this challenge, offering the same cutting-edge performance but with a focus on efficiency, affordability, and open access for anyone who wanted to engage with AI technology.

Limitations of Existing AI Models

Despite the impressive capabilities of models like GPT-4 and Nvidia's deep learning frameworks, limitations were starting to show. First, there was the cost—these models were incredibly resource-intensive, requiring both powerful hardware and immense data sets to train. Smaller companies couldn't afford to compete at that scale, and even large organizations were feeling the strain of mounting infrastructure costs. Additionally, the models themselves, while highly capable, were often black boxes—difficult for users to fully understand, interpret, or modify for their own specific needs. The lack of transparency and flexibility in these systems created a sense of frustration among many in the AI community.

Furthermore, as the AI landscape became more fragmented, the need for multimodal models—systems that could seamlessly handle various tasks like image generation, text interpretation, and even audio processing—became more pressing. Existing models were typically designed for specific tasks, and integrating them into larger systems was both time-consuming and expensive. Janus Pro's innovative unified architecture broke down these barriers, offering a model that could handle diverse tasks all in one place.

The Demand for a More Efficient and Open-Source AI

As AI development continued, there was a growing consensus among researchers and developers alike: the time had come for a new wave of innovation—one that prioritized accessibility, transparency, and efficiency. The demand for an open-source model that didn't require deep pockets to develop or deploy became louder, as did the call for an AI system that was not just powerful but also adaptable to the needs of individual users and smaller companies.

Janus Pro answered this call with a revolutionary approach. By making their model open-source, DeepSeek removed the barriers to entry that had previously limited access to

AI. This wasn't just about building a more powerful model—it was about creating an inclusive ecosystem where innovation could flourish without the constraints imposed by expensive licenses or proprietary systems. Janus Pro's combination of performance, affordability, and openness offered a glimpse into a future where AI could be harnessed by anyone with the right ideas and the will to experiment.

Chapter 2

Introducing Janus Pro: DeepSeek's Bold Innovation

The world of artificial intelligence has always been driven by competition. Every few years, a new breakthrough shifts the balance, setting new standards for what's possible. But until now, those breakthroughs had always come from the same familiar names—tech giants with vast resources, deep pockets, and tight control over the AI ecosystem. Then, seemingly out of nowhere, came DeepSeek's

Janus Pro, a disruptive force that sent shockwaves through the AI industry.

Janus Pro wasn't just another AI model; it was a statement, a declaration that powerful artificial intelligence didn't have to be locked behind closed doors or reserved for billion-dollar corporations. In an industry where exclusivity and high barriers to entry had long been the norm, DeepSeek had done the unthinkable: they built a cutting-edge AI model that rivaled the best of OpenAI and Nvidia—at a fraction of the cost.

The mere announcement of Janus Pro sent ripples through the AI community. How had a relatively lesser-known company built something that could compete with GPT-4 and DALL·E 3? How had they developed an AI system that performed on par with, or even outperformed, models backed by Silicon Valley's biggest players?

The answer lay not just in DeepSeek's vision but in its willingness to challenge the status quo. This was not just about building another AI model. It was about rethinking AI itself—how it was created, who had access to it, and what it could truly achieve in the hands of a global community.

What is Janus Pro?

At its core, Janus Pro is a multimodal AI model—a system designed to understand and process multiple types of data, including text, images, and more. Unlike traditional models that specialize in just one area, Janus Pro seamlessly blends capabilities. It can generate human-like text, analyze complex images, and even integrate insights across different types of data—all in a single system.

But what made Janus Pro truly stand out wasn't just its versatility. It was the fact that DeepSeek had achieved this level of performance with a model developed at a fraction of the cost of its competitors. While companies like OpenAI and Google had spent hundreds of millions of dollars training their latest models, DeepSeek had done it with a budget reportedly under six million dollars—a number that seemed almost impossible in the world of advanced AI research.

This raised an immediate question: If DeepSeek could build a world-class AI for a fraction of the cost, why were Silicon Valley companies spending so much more?

That question alone was enough to turn heads.

But the real shock came when benchmarks and performance tests began rolling in. In evaluations like GenEval and DPG-Bench, Janus Pro was going head-to-head with the most powerful AI models on the planet—and in some cases, it was winning.

Suddenly, the narrative had shifted. Janus Pro wasn't just a budget-friendly alternative to big tech's AI models—it was a contender.

A new player had entered the game, and the industry was paying attention.

The Vision Behind DeepSeek's AI Model

Every great innovation begins with a vision, and Janus Pro was no exception.

DeepSeek didn't just want to build a powerful AI model. They wanted to redefine what was possible in AI development. Their approach was guided by three fundamental principles:

Efficiency: Build an AI model that could achieve cutting-edge performance without requiring hundreds of millions of dollars in compute resources.

Accessibility: Create a system that wasn't locked behind paywalls, allowing researchers, startups, and independent developers to harness its capabilities.

Open Collaboration: Challenge the traditional model of AI research by making key aspects of Janus Pro open-source, inviting a global community to innovate together.

This vision was in stark contrast to how companies like OpenAI, Google, and Nvidia approached AI. While those companies prioritized commercial applications and corporate partnerships, DeepSeek wanted to democratize AI.

They weren't just asking, "How can we make the best AI?"

They were asking, "How can we make AI that's for everyone?"

This approach wasn't just disruptive—it was revolutionary. It meant that for the first time, cutting-edge AI wouldn't be restricted to those with billion-dollar budgets. It would be available to anyone with the vision and creativity to use it.

That idea alone was enough to make AI enthusiasts, researchers, and developers worldwide take notice.

Key Features That Set Janus Pro Apart

So, what exactly made Janus Pro different?

While many AI models claimed to be powerful and multimodal, Janus Pro delivered in a way that few had before.

1. A Unified Transformer Architecture

Most AI models today are trained separately for different tasks. Language models like GPT-4 focus on text, while image models like DALL·E handle visuals. But Janus Pro combined everything into a single, unified architecture, allowing it to process and generate both text and images seamlessly.

This approach meant that Janus Pro could analyze an image and write about it in the same breath—a level of integration that even the best AI models struggled to achieve.

2. Unmatched Cost Efficiency

One of the biggest shocks in the AI industry was learning that DeepSeek had built Janus Pro with a budget under six million dollars.

By optimizing their training process and developing more efficient model architectures, DeepSeek proved that AI development didn't have to be an arms race of spending.

This breakthrough opened doors for smaller AI startups and researchers who previously thought high-end AI development was out of reach.

3. Open-Source Accessibility

Unlike other AI giants that closely guarded their models, DeepSeek made a bold move: They opened up key aspects of Janus Pro for public access.

This meant that instead of relying solely on big corporations for innovation, the global AI community could now experiment with, refine, and expand upon Janus Pro's capabilities.

It wasn't just a model—it was an invitation to collaborate.

4. Competitive Performance on AI Benchmarks

Janus Pro wasn't just affordable and open-source—it was powerful.

It ranked impressively in AI benchmarks like GenEval and DPG-Bench, standing toe-to-toe with the best models from OpenAI, Google, and Nvidia.

For many, this was the proof that DeepSeek wasn't just making bold claims—it was delivering results.

A Disruptive Force in AI

With its release, Janus Pro reshaped the AI landscape overnight.

No longer was advanced AI reserved for a handful of tech giants. No longer was cutting-edge innovation locked behind billion-dollar budgets.

DeepSeek had done something no one thought possible: they built an AI model that was powerful, efficient, and accessible—and in doing so, they challenged everything the industry thought it knew about AI development.

The question now wasn't whether Janus Pro could compete with the biggest names in AI.

It was how soon the rest of the world would catch up to what DeepSeek had just unleashed.

Chapter 3

How Janus Pro Works: The Technology Behind the Model

The world of artificial intelligence had long been defined by one simple equation: better performance meant higher costs, bigger models, and more computational power. Every advancement in AI seemed to demand an exponential increase in data, processing, and money.

Then came Janus Pro—a model that rewrote the rules.

Unlike the AI models before it, Janus Pro didn't need billion-dollar budgets or massive server farms to achieve cutting-edge performance. It could match, and in some cases surpass, the capabilities of GPT-4 and other leading models—at a fraction of the cost.

How was this possible?

At the core of Janus Pro's success was an innovative approach to architecture, multimodal capabilities, and efficiency—a combination that allowed it to compete with the biggest players without the usual trade-offs.

Understanding Janus Pro's Unified Transformer Architecture

Artificial intelligence had long been built on a fragmented system. Language models like GPT-4 were trained specifically for text, while image models like Stable Diffusion or DALL·E specialized in visuals. Each system worked in isolation, designed for one purpose alone.

But Janus Pro changed that paradigm.

Instead of training separate models for different tasks, DeepSeek developed a Unified Transformer Architecture—a single, seamless

28

system that could process and generate both text and images with equal fluency.

This breakthrough meant that Janus Pro didn't just "understand" words the way traditional AI models did. It could see, interpret, and reason across multiple types of data—all within a single framework.

Imagine asking an AI to describe a picture, analyze a historical document, and write a short story—all without switching models or sacrificing performance.

That was the power of Janus Pro.

This unified approach also eliminated redundancies in training, making the model vastly more efficient than its predecessors. Instead of requiring separate neural networks for different tasks, Janus Pro streamlined the process—leading to faster inference times, reduced computational costs, and better adaptability across different AI applications.

DeepSeek had essentially broken down the barriers between AI modalities, creating a model that functioned more like a true general intelligence rather than a collection of specialized tools.

Multimodal Capabilities: Text, Image, and Beyond

For years, AI had been impressive—but limited. Language models like GPT-4 could generate human-like text, but they couldn't see or interpret images in the way humans could. Meanwhile, image-generation models like Midjourney or DALL·E could create stunning visuals but had no understanding of language beyond simple prompts.

Janus Pro merged these worlds.

It wasn't just a text model. It wasn't just an image model. It was both—and more.

This meant it could:

Generate detailed, context-aware images based on complex text prompts

Analyze and describe images with near-human accuracy

Combine textual and visual reasoning to solve problems that required both modalities

For example, if you showed Janus Pro an ancient map, it wouldn't just recognize it as a map. It could:

Describe its historical significance

Compare it to modern geography

Analyze its artistic style and origins

This multimodal approach allowed Janus Pro to handle real-world tasks far more effectively than previous AI models.

It could process graphs, charts, diagrams, and even handwritten notes, making it invaluable for education, research, and business applications.

Perhaps most impressively, Janus Pro was designed to adapt.

While other models struggled with context switching—moving between different types of input and output—Janus Pro handled the transition smoothly. This ability to understand, interpret, and generate across multiple domains was something few AI systems had ever achieved.

It was the closest thing yet to a truly multimodal AI—one that could interact with the world in ways no previous model had done before.

Efficiency vs. Cost: Achieving GPT-4-Like Results for Less

In the AI industry, performance often comes at a cost—a massive one.

Training and running advanced AI models require hundreds of millions of dollars, often putting cutting-edge AI research out of reach for smaller companies, researchers, and independent developers.

Janus Pro shattered that notion.

Despite its incredible capabilities, Janus Pro was built on an astonishingly low budget compared to its competitors. While companies like OpenAI and Google poured hundreds of millions into training, DeepSeek created a model that could compete for under six million dollars.

How?

1. Smarter Training Methods

Janus Pro used data-efficient training techniques that reduced the need for excessive compute power.

Instead of relying solely on massive datasets, DeepSeek optimized how the model learned, using advanced reinforcement learning and knowledge distillation techniques.

2. Optimized Model Architecture

By designing a more efficient neural network, Janus Pro achieved high-level performance without requiring excessive hardware.

This meant it could run on cheaper, more accessible GPUs, making deployment far more affordable than traditional AI models.

3. Scalability Without Complexity

Many AI models struggle to scale efficiently—requiring enormous resources as they grow larger.

Janus Pro's architecture was designed to scale smoothly, allowing it to handle increased workloads without exponentially increasing costs.

The result?

A model that could rival GPT-4 and other top-tier AI systems while being dramatically more cost-effective.

This breakthrough had profound implications:

Startups and independent developers could now build powerful AI applications without needing Silicon Valley budgets.

Researchers and universities could access state-of-the-art AI without relying on Big Tech partnerships.

Businesses could integrate high-level AI into their operations without facing astronomical costs.

DeepSeek had democratized AI in a way that few thought possible.

A Game-Changer for AI Development

Janus Pro wasn't just an improvement over existing models—it was a fundamental shift in AI technology.

By combining:

A Unified Transformer Architecture

True multimodal capabilities

Unprecedented efficiency and cost-effectiveness

DeepSeek had created one of the most advanced AI models of its time—without following the traditional, resource-heavy approach.

For the first time, AI development wasn't just about bigger budgets and bigger models.

It was about smarter design, open access, and breaking barriers.

Janus Pro proved that AI could be powerful, affordable, and accessible—a vision that was already reshaping the future of artificial intelligence.

And as the world began to realize the full potential of this new model, one thing became clear:

The AI landscape would never be the same again.

Chapter 4

Janus Pro vs. The Competition: A Performance Breakdown

In the fast-moving world of artificial intelligence, performance is everything.

An AI model's success isn't just about how well it generates text or images, but how efficiently and reliably it performs under real-world conditions. Speed, accuracy, adaptability—these are the factors that determine whether a model becomes an industry leader or fades into obscurity.

Janus Pro entered the AI race as a direct challenger to OpenAI's GPT-4 and DALL-E 3, Google's Gemini, and Anthropic's Claude models. Each of these systems had established itself as a powerhouse in AI generation, yet they all had limitations—whether in cost, accessibility, or functionality.

DeepSeek's ambition wasn't just to match these existing models—it was to outperform them where it mattered most.

Janus Pro wasn't just another AI—it was built to be more efficient, more flexible, and more affordable than the competition.

But how does it truly compare?

A closer look at its performance across benchmarks and real-world applications reveals a model that isn't just competing—it's redefining the AI landscape.

How It Compares to OpenAI's DALL-E 3 and GPT-4

For years, OpenAI had dominated the AI space with models like GPT-4 for text generation and DALL-E 3 for image creation. These models were cutting-edge, capable of producing highly detailed responses and stunning visuals.

Yet they came with significant trade-offs.

1. High Costs:

OpenAI's most advanced models required substantial financial resources, making them less accessible to smaller businesses, startups, and independent developers.

GPT-4's API, for instance, was far more expensive per token than earlier models, while DALL-E 3's image generation often came with usage restrictions and pricing limitations.

2. Limited Accessibility & Control:

OpenAI controlled who could use their models and how they could be applied.

Developers had to rely on OpenAI's API, meaning they had limited ability to fine-tune or customize the models for specific use cases.

3. Performance Bottlenecks:

While powerful, GPT-4 suffered from response latency issues, particularly when generating long-form content.

DALL-E 3, despite its impressive image generation, still struggled with fine details and multi-element compositions, often misinterpreting complex prompts.

Janus Pro addressed each of these weaknesses head-on.

Affordability: Janus Pro was designed to match GPT-4's capabilities at a fraction of the cost, making high-level AI more accessible than ever before.

Customizability: Unlike OpenAI's models, Janus Pro wasn't locked behind a restrictive API—it could be fine-tuned and integrated into private systems.

Speed & Efficiency: With its optimized architecture, Janus Pro ran inference tasks faster, allowing users to generate text and images with minimal delay.

In direct text-generation comparisons, Janus Pro's responses were:

More concise and accurate than GPT-4 in technical and factual tasks

More flexible in creative storytelling, adapting better to different writing styles

Faster in generating long-form content, avoiding the lag that plagued GPT-4 users

For image generation, early tests showed that Janus Pro matched or even surpassed DALL-E 3 in realism, composition, and coherence, particularly in handling complex prompts with multiple elements.

By addressing the major weaknesses of OpenAI's models, DeepSeek positioned Janus Pro as a true alternative—one that didn't just compete on performance but offered greater efficiency, lower costs, and more control to users.

Benchmarks and Testing: GenEval, DPG-Bench, and More

Numbers don't lie.

When evaluating AI models, researchers use benchmark tests to measure performance in areas like language understanding, reasoning, image generation, and efficiency.

Janus Pro was put through a series of rigorous industry-standard tests to determine how it stacked up against its competitors.

1. GenEval:

A benchmark designed to test AI's ability to reason, summarize, and generate coherent, accurate responses.

Janus Pro consistently scored at or above GPT-4 levels in tasks that required deep contextual understanding.

2. DPG-Bench:

A dataset measuring multimodal AI performance, assessing how well a model handles both text and image-based reasoning.

Janus Pro's image-text alignment accuracy was higher than DALL-E 3's, particularly in object placement, realism, and artistic composition.

3. Human Evaluation Metrics:

Unlike traditional benchmarks, which rely on automated scoring, Janus Pro was also tested through direct human comparison.

Across thousands of user interactions, Janus Pro's responses were rated as more natural, contextually aware, and engaging than other models.

These results weren't just impressive—they proved that Janus Pro was capable of competing at the highest levels of AI performance.

But raw performance is only part of the equation.

Where AI truly matters is real-world application—how it performs outside of controlled testing environments.

Real-World Applications and Strengths

For AI to be valuable, it needs to work where it matters most: in business, research, content creation, and everyday problem-solving.

Janus Pro's unique combination of speed, accuracy, and multimodal capabilities made it an ideal choice for industries seeking powerful AI solutions without the high costs of traditional models.

Some of its strongest real-world applications included:

Business Automation:

Companies could use Janus Pro for customer support, market analysis, and workflow optimization, improving efficiency while reducing operational costs.

Creative Industries:

Writers, designers, and artists found that Janus Pro provided more flexible, creative output than GPT-4, generating better storylines, character development, and visual art.

Scientific & Academic Research:

Universities and research institutions used Janus Pro to analyze complex data, generate reports, and even assist in AI-driven scientific discovery.

Healthcare & Diagnostics:

With its multimodal processing, Janus Pro was able to interpret medical images and analyze clinical text—offering potential breakthroughs in AI-assisted medicine.

In each of these sectors, the key advantage of Janus Pro was accessibility.

Unlike GPT-4 or DALL-E 3, which required expensive API access and external hosting, Janus Pro could be self-hosted, fine-tuned, and scaled to meet specific needs—making it one of the most versatile AI models available.

The verdict was clear.

Janus Pro didn't just compete with OpenAI's best models—it often exceeded them in efficiency, cost, and adaptability.

For businesses, developers, and AI enthusiasts looking for a high-performance model without the constraints of Big Tech, Janus Pro wasn't just an alternative—it was the smarter choice.

Chapter 5

The Open-Source Advantage

Artificial intelligence is shaping the future, yet a critical battle is unfolding behind the scenes—a battle between open-source innovation and corporate control.

For decades, technological progress has thrived on the principles of open collaboration, shared knowledge, and unrestricted access. From the early days of software development to the rise of the internet, breakthroughs were often driven by communities rather than corporations.

Yet, as AI evolved into one of the most powerful tools of the 21st century, Big Tech companies seized control, placing restrictions on access, monetizing every interaction, and creating walled gardens where only a select few could benefit.

DeepSeek's Janus Pro represents a radical shift in this landscape. By embracing open-source principles, it challenges the status quo, offering an alternative to closed models controlled by tech giants.

This movement isn't just about giving people access to better AI—it's about democratizing intelligence itself.

Why Open-Source AI Matters

The open-source philosophy isn't new, but in the realm of artificial intelligence, it has taken on unprecedented significance.

1. Accessibility for All, Not Just Corporations

Open-source AI removes financial and technical barriers, allowing researchers, small businesses, and developers to access cutting-edge models without needing massive budgets.

Unlike proprietary models like GPT-4 or Google's Gemini, which require costly API access and corporate approval, Janus Pro is built for anyone to use, modify, and improve.

2. Faster Innovation Through Collective Intelligence

Proprietary AI models evolve within the limits of corporate research teams, whereas open-source projects harness global talent.

Thousands of developers can spot flaws, contribute improvements, and push the technology forward faster than a closed team ever could.

3. Transparency and Trust

Closed-source AI models operate in a black box—users have no way to verify biases, security risks, or hidden limitations.

Open-source AI like Janus Pro allows complete transparency, meaning developers and researchers can audit the code, assess biases, and ensure ethical use.

4. Customization and Flexibility

Businesses relying on proprietary AI models must accept whatever features and restrictions the provider imposes.

Open-source AI empowers companies to fine-tune models for their specific needs, ensuring greater efficiency and better results.

The question isn't why open-source AI matters—it's why Big Tech is so determined to keep AI locked away.

How DeepSeek is Challenging Big Tech's Closed Models

For years, AI development was dominated by a handful of companies—OpenAI, Google, Meta, and Microsoft—each racing to create the most powerful proprietary models.

Their strategy was simple:

Control the data

Restrict access

Monetize usage

This approach turned AI into a luxury service rather than a shared resource, forcing businesses and developers to pay for access without control over the technology itself.

DeepSeek's Janus Pro is built on an entirely different premise:

AI should be an open, evolving tool available to all

Innovation should be driven by global collaboration, not corporate interests

The power of AI should be in the hands of the people, not a select few

By releasing Janus Pro as an open-source model, DeepSeek is disrupting the status quo in three major ways:

1. Freeing Developers from Costly APIs

OpenAI's GPT-4 API comes with pricing structures that scale based on usage, making it unaffordable for smaller projects.

Janus Pro allows developers to host their own instances, eliminating the need to rely on expensive third-party services.

2. Enabling Independent AI Research

AI researchers working with closed models have to operate within strict guidelines set by tech companies.

With Janus Pro, researchers can modify, test, and improve the AI without restrictions, leading to faster breakthroughs and discoveries.

3. Promoting Ethical AI Development

Companies like Google and OpenAI have faced criticism for opaque moderation policies and built-in biases.

Open-source AI allows the community to detect and correct biases, ensuring AI remains fair, ethical, and unbiased.

This shift isn't just about competing with Big Tech—it's about redefining the very foundations of AI development.

Implications for Developers and the AI Community

The rise of open-source AI models like Janus Pro is reshaping the landscape for developers, businesses, and researchers.

Developers Gain More Freedom

Instead of being locked into expensive API services, developers can build, customize, and scale AI solutions on their own terms.

Open-source AI means no restrictions on modifications, allowing developers to tailor models for niche applications.

Startups and Businesses Save Costs

Proprietary AI models force businesses to pay for access, increasing operational costs.

With Janus Pro, companies can run AI locally, eliminating recurring fees and data privacy concerns.

A More Ethical and Transparent AI Future

By opening AI development to the global community, biases and security risks can be identified and addressed more quickly.

Governments and regulatory bodies will find it easier to assess AI risks and ensure responsible development.

The implications of open-source AI extend far beyond cost savings or technical advantages—they represent a shift in power from corporations to individuals, from closed networks to open collaboration.

DeepSeek's commitment to open-source AI isn't just a business decision—it's a revolution in how artificial intelligence is built, shared, and used.

And with Janus Pro leading the way, the future of AI isn't in the hands of a few—it's in the hands of everyone.

Chapter 6

The Economic Impact of Janus Pro

Artificial intelligence has long been a game-changing force across industries, but its rapid progress has come at a cost—both figuratively and literally. The development and deployment of large-scale AI models require massive computational power, vast datasets, and ongoing financial investment.

For years, major AI companies have invested billions into creating proprietary models, passing the costs onto users through expensive API subscriptions, licensing fees, and closed-source restrictions. This has excluded smaller businesses, researchers, and independent developers from fully utilizing AI's potential, creating an industry dominated by a few tech giants.

DeepSeek's Janus Pro is rewriting the economic landscape of AI by offering high-performance capabilities at a fraction of the cost. Instead of following the traditional model of monetizing AI through restrictive pricing, Janus Pro embraces open-source accessibility, lower infrastructure demands, and cost-efficient optimization.

The financial implications of this shift extend far beyond DeepSeek itself—Janus Pro is reshaping AI affordability, altering development budgets, and forcing a reassessment of research funding strategies.

How DeepSeek Achieved High Performance at a Fraction of the Cost

Building a state-of-the-art AI model typically involves enormous expenditures, from acquiring high-quality training data to securing computational resources capable of handling deep learning at scale.

Tech companies like OpenAI, Google, and Meta have relied on multi-billion-dollar budgets to train and refine their models. OpenAI's GPT-4, for example, required an immense cloud infrastructure and proprietary datasets, making it an expensive project that demanded high monetization to recoup costs.

DeepSeek, however, took a different approach, leveraging three key economic strategies to keep costs low while maintaining high performance:

1. Optimized Model Architecture for Efficiency

Traditional AI models prioritize sheer scale, increasing parameter counts and computational intensity to improve results.

Janus Pro achieves similar capabilities by refining its Unified Transformer Architecture, reducing unnecessary complexity while maximizing efficiency.

This optimization allows Janus Pro to deliver GPT-4-like results without requiring an equivalent computational footprint.

2. Leveraging Open-Source Contributions

Instead of relying on in-house research alone, DeepSeek benefits from global collaboration through its open-source model.

Thousands of researchers and developers contribute improvements, eliminating the need for expensive proprietary research teams.

This approach mirrors successful open-source projects like Linux, which have flourished through decentralized development.

3. Reducing Infrastructure Dependence

Major AI firms operate through cloud-based APIs, requiring them to maintain massive server farms and data centers.

Janus Pro allows developers to run AI locally or on their own hardware, reducing reliance on third-party infrastructure and lowering operational costs for both DeepSeek and its users.

By focusing on efficiency, collaboration, and decentralization, DeepSeek has demonstrated that world-class AI does not have to come with world-class expenses.

The Financial Implications for AI Development

The introduction of Janus Pro has triggered a shift in the financial dynamics of AI development. Traditionally, creating an AI model required:

1. Expensive Licensing Fees for Proprietary Models

Companies developing AI applications had to pay for access to closed models like GPT-4 or Claude.

With Janus Pro's open-source accessibility, developers can integrate AI without ongoing costs.

2. High Cloud Computing Costs

Training AI models requires powerful GPUs and extensive cloud infrastructure.

By designing Janus Pro to be lightweight and efficient, DeepSeek allows companies to reduce reliance on cloud providers, saving millions in computational expenses.

3. Increased Competition and Price Reductions

Open-source AI models put pressure on major tech firms to lower their prices, as businesses now have free alternatives.

This creates a more competitive market, benefiting startups and smaller enterprises that previously couldn't afford AI integration.

The financial ripple effect of Janus Pro's cost efficiency extends beyond businesses—it is forcing a reassessment of AI investment strategies on a global scale.

Rethinking AI Research Budgets and Funding
Strategies

Historically, AI research has been funded
through a combination of:

Corporate-backed investments (OpenAI's
partnership with Microsoft)

Government grants (U.S. and EU funding for AI
research)

Venture capital funding for startups

With Janus Pro lowering the financial barriers
to entry, organizations must reevaluate how AI
projects are funded and developed.

1. Democratization of AI Research

Universities and independent researchers
previously struggled with funding, as accessing
AI models required expensive cloud resources.

Open-source models like Janus Pro remove
this barrier, allowing AI research to flourish
outside of corporate labs.

2. Shifting Investment Focus

Instead of pouring billions into proprietary AI models, companies are now investing in customizing and fine-tuning open-source solutions.

This shift allows for more targeted innovation, reducing wasted funding on redundant AI development.

3. A New Era of AI Startups

The high costs of AI development previously limited entry to well-funded startups.

With lower barriers to AI integration, smaller companies can now compete with industry giants without needing enormous capital.

DeepSeek's economic strategy isn't just about reducing costs—it's about leveling the playing field. By making AI development financially viable for everyone, Janus Pro is accelerating innovation while challenging traditional funding models.

Chapter 7

AI Disruption: How Janus Pro is Shaping the Future

Artificial intelligence has undergone an extraordinary transformation over the last decade, evolving from niche research projects to the backbone of industries worldwide. From natural language processing and image generation to automation and decision-making, AI has become an integral force in modern life. However, its widespread adoption has also brought challenges—rising costs, ethical concerns, and increasing control by tech monopolies.

For years, companies like OpenAI, Google DeepMind, and Meta have dictated the trajectory of AI development, locking innovations behind paywalls and proprietary frameworks. Access to cutting-edge AI required substantial financial resources, leaving startups, researchers, and independent developers struggling to keep pace.

Janus Pro, developed by DeepSeek, is disrupting this model. By delivering high-performance AI at a fraction of the cost, it is reshaping the industry, breaking monopolies, and redefining accessibility. More than just a powerful AI model, Janus Pro is a catalyst for global transformation, forcing competitors to rethink their strategies and opening doors for broader participation in AI research and application.

As this technology gains momentum, it is sparking market reactions, industry shifts, and global implications. But with disruption comes challenges—ethical dilemmas, regulatory concerns, and potential misuse. Understanding these dynamics is crucial to grasping how Janus Pro is shaping the future of AI.

Market Reactions and Industry Shifts

The introduction of Janus Pro has sent shockwaves across the AI landscape.

Traditional players—OpenAI, Google, Microsoft, and Anthropic—have built their business models around high-cost, subscription-based AI services, requiring enterprises and developers to pay for access to advanced models like GPT-4, Claude, and Gemini.

Janus Pro challenges this paradigm, offering comparable capabilities without the heavy financial burden. This has triggered significant shifts in how companies, developers, and industries approach AI adoption.

1. Competition and Pricing Pressure

Before Janus Pro, AI development was dominated by a handful of companies that dictated pricing structures and access levels. These firms invested billions into training proprietary models and justified their steep costs through exclusivity.

OpenAI's GPT-4 API costs can run into thousands of dollars per month for enterprise-level usage.

Google's Gemini models are tied to Google Cloud services, forcing businesses into their ecosystem.

Microsoft and Anthropic offer AI through tiered pricing, limiting access based on subscription levels.

With Janus Pro providing comparable AI capabilities at a fraction of the cost, these companies are now under pressure to rethink their pricing models.

Potential response strategies:

Lowering API prices to remain competitive.

Introducing open-source alternatives to counter Janus Pro's appeal.

Shifting revenue models toward custom AI solutions and consulting rather than direct model licensing.

This disruption benefits businesses, startups, and independent developers, who now have more choices when integrating AI.

2. AI Democratization and Increased Adoption

High AI costs previously limited access to major corporations and well-funded tech startups. Many small businesses, educators, and independent researchers were locked out of advanced AI capabilities due to prohibitive pricing.

Janus Pro is reversing this trend by making AI widely accessible and affordable, leading to:

Greater adoption in smaller businesses for automation, customer service, and content creation.

Expanded AI use in education, allowing universities and students to experiment with advanced models.

Broader research participation, as independent AI developers can now access top-tier models without financial barriers.

This shift is reminiscent of the open-source revolution in software development, where projects like Linux and Python paved the way for widespread tech adoption outside of corporate control.

3. Corporate Resistance and Adaptation

While some companies are embracing Janus Pro's disruption, others are taking defensive positions to maintain market dominance.

Proprietary AI firms may seek to reinforce their influence by:

Enhancing security and proprietary features unavailable in open-source models.

Tightening AI licensing agreements to discourage alternatives.

Influencing policymakers to introduce regulations favoring closed AI models.

Despite resistance, the momentum of open AI adoption is accelerating, making it increasingly difficult for proprietary models to maintain their dominance without significant innovation or cost reductions.

The Global Impact on AI Development

Janus Pro's disruption is not confined to tech giants—it is reshaping global AI research, economic opportunities, and policy discussions.

1. Accelerating AI Research and Innovation

Previously, groundbreaking AI research was concentrated in wealthy nations with access to high-end computing resources. Countries and organizations with limited budgets struggled to keep pace, leading to a widening technological gap.

Janus Pro is bridging this divide by offering a low-cost, high-performance alternative, enabling:

Universities in developing nations to conduct AI research without reliance on expensive cloud services.

Independent AI labs to experiment with models on affordable hardware.

Entrepreneurs worldwide to integrate AI into products without requiring multimillion-dollar funding.

2. Reshaping the AI Job Market

The affordability and accessibility of Janus Pro mean that AI expertise is no longer restricted to large corporations. As AI adoption spreads:

Demand for AI specialists will rise in smaller firms and emerging markets.

More businesses will develop AI-driven products, leading to new job creation in automation, AI ethics, and deployment.

Workforce adaptation will accelerate, as AI-powered tools become commonplace in content creation, coding, and business operations.

3. Influencing AI Policy and Regulation

Government bodies worldwide are monitoring AI's rapid expansion, with debates surrounding:

Ethical AI deployment

Regulatory compliance for AI-generated content

Intellectual property protection

As Janus Pro removes financial barriers, regulators will face new challenges in ensuring responsible AI use without stifling innovation.

Potential Challenges and Ethical Considerations

Janus Pro's impact is overwhelmingly positive, but its disruptive nature also presents challenges that must be addressed.

1. Misuse and Ethical Concerns

Open-source AI models, while democratizing, increase the risk of misuse in areas such as:

Deepfake generation and misinformation

Automated hacking and cyber threats

Bias and discrimination in AI applications

2. Sustainability and Funding for Open AI

While Janus Pro offers AI at a lower cost, ongoing development requires funding. Open-source models must find sustainable revenue streams to support continuous improvement.

3. Intellectual Property and Data Integrity

As AI models become widespread, ensuring transparency and ethical data usage is critical. Policymakers and developers must work together to establish guidelines for responsible AI deployment.

Chapter 8

The Future of DeepSeek and Janus Pro

The rapid evolution of artificial intelligence has been driven by a handful of key players, each competing to develop the most advanced and efficient models. While large corporations like OpenAI, Google DeepMind, and Anthropic have dominated the AI space with proprietary models, a growing movement toward open-source AI development is shifting the balance of power.

DeepSeek's Janus Pro has emerged as a groundbreaking force, challenging closed AI models by offering a high-performance alternative at a fraction of the cost. The model's accessibility has reshaped AI development, research, and business strategies, ensuring that advanced AI is not limited to a few major corporations.

As DeepSeek continues its journey, several questions arise: What's next for Janus Pro? How will DeepSeek expand its capabilities? What long-term impact will this AI model have on the industry? The future of DeepSeek and Janus Pro will determine how AI is developed, implemented, and regulated in the coming years.

What's Next for DeepSeek?

DeepSeek's success with Janus Pro has positioned it as a major disruptor in the AI landscape, but maintaining momentum requires continuous innovation. With increasing competition and growing industry expectations, DeepSeek is likely to focus on three major areas: model improvement, industry adoption, and strategic partnerships.

1. Enhancing Janus Pro's Architecture

The AI industry moves at an unprecedented pace, with new breakthroughs in machine learning, model efficiency, and computational optimization emerging frequently. To stay ahead, DeepSeek must:

Optimize computational efficiency to ensure Janus Pro remains cost-effective for developers.

Improve context length and reasoning capabilities to match or surpass models like GPT-4 and Gemini.

Refine natural language understanding to enhance usability across industries, from customer service to content creation.

2. Expanding Open-Source Collaboration

One of Janus Pro's biggest advantages is its open-source foundation, allowing researchers and developers worldwide to contribute to improvements and build upon the model. DeepSeek may encourage:

Community-driven enhancements, similar to how open-source projects like Linux and PyTorch have thrived through collective contributions.

Transparent development roadmaps, enabling AI researchers to suggest and implement modifications.

Decentralized AI improvements, reducing reliance on any single company for technological progress.

3. Strategic Partnerships and Integrations

To maximize impact, DeepSeek will likely seek collaborations with industry leaders, cloud providers, and research institutions. Potential directions include:

Partnerships with cloud computing firms to integrate Janus Pro into cost-effective AI infrastructure.

Collaboration with universities to promote AI research and ethical development.

Integration with business applications, allowing enterprises to incorporate AI without excessive costs.

These efforts will determine how DeepSeek remains competitive in an environment where tech giants continuously refine their models.

Expanding Janus Pro's Capabilities

AI models must evolve continuously to meet new challenges and demands. As industries integrate AI at a larger scale, expectations for speed, accuracy, and adaptability grow. Expanding Janus Pro's capabilities will require innovation across multiple dimensions.

1. Advancing Multimodal AI

The next frontier of AI lies in multimodal capabilities—the ability to process and generate text, images, audio, and video simultaneously. Companies like OpenAI and Google have begun developing multimodal models, and DeepSeek must follow suit to remain competitive.

Potential enhancements include:

Image and text generation fusion, allowing users to generate detailed visual content based on textual prompts.

Audio synthesis and understanding, enabling advanced speech recognition and AI-generated voice applications.

Real-time AI interaction, creating models that seamlessly switch between different input types for greater versatility.

2. Improving Real-World Decision-Making

AI is no longer confined to research labs—it is actively shaping finance, healthcare, cybersecurity, and business strategy. To remain relevant, Janus Pro must enhance its ability to analyze data, predict trends, and assist in complex decision-making.

Areas of focus may include:

Stronger contextual reasoning, enabling AI to provide more insightful and nuanced responses.

Predictive analytics, helping businesses and researchers forecast trends based on vast datasets.

AI-driven automation, allowing organizations to streamline operations without excessive costs.

3. Strengthening AI Safety and Ethics

With AI models becoming increasingly powerful, safety and ethical concerns are at the forefront of discussion. DeepSeek must ensure that Janus Pro remains:

Bias-free, preventing skewed results or discriminatory outputs.

Transparent, offering clear documentation on data sources and training methodologies.

Compliant with global AI regulations, adapting to evolving policies on AI governance.

By expanding Janus Pro's capabilities while maintaining trust, safety, and efficiency, DeepSeek can solidify its position as a leader in ethical AI development.

The Long-Term Influence on AI Innovation

The impact of Janus Pro extends far beyond DeepSeek—it has the potential to reshape the AI industry in ways that will be felt for years.

1. Redefining AI Accessibility

For decades, AI development has been dominated by well-funded corporations with access to massive computing resources. Janus Pro disrupts this model by proving that high-performance AI does not have to be locked behind paywalls.

Over time, this shift may:

Encourage more open-source AI projects, reducing dependency on tech monopolies.

Promote AI adoption in developing countries, where expensive proprietary models were previously a barrier.

Drive innovation from independent developers, who can now build upon advanced AI models without massive budgets.

2. Shaping Future AI Business Models

With affordable, open AI models gaining traction, companies relying on premium AI services will need to adjust their strategies. Future business models may focus on:

Custom AI solutions rather than universal APIs.

AI-powered tools and applications instead of direct model licensing.

Hybrid approaches, where proprietary models integrate with open-source innovations.

The ripple effect of Janus Pro's affordability will force AI providers to rethink their monetization strategies, leading to greater consumer choice and industry diversity.

3. Accelerating AI Regulation and Ethics Discussions

AI development is moving faster than regulatory frameworks, prompting concerns over misuse, bias, and ethical implications. As Janus Pro expands AI accessibility, policymakers will need to:

Establish clearer AI safety standards, ensuring responsible development.

Address concerns about misinformation and deepfake technology, which open models could exacerbate.

Create guidelines for AI accountability, particularly in sensitive industries like healthcare and finance.

By leading the charge in responsible, open-source AI, DeepSeek has the opportunity to set ethical standards for the industry while proving that accessibility and safety can coexist.

Conclusion

The development of Janus Pro marks a transformative moment in the history of artificial intelligence. While AI advancements have historically been driven by well-funded corporations, the emergence of cost-effective, high-performance models like Janus Pro is redefining industry standards. DeepSeek has demonstrated that open-source AI can not only rival but, in some cases, outperform proprietary models—pushing the boundaries of accessibility, affordability, and innovation.

With AI adoption increasing across industries, the future of artificial intelligence is no longer solely dictated by tech giants. Instead, researchers, developers, and businesses of all sizes are gaining access to powerful AI capabilities, reshaping how AI is used, regulated, and monetized. Janus Pro has set the stage for a new era in AI development, one where efficiency, transparency, and inclusivity play a more significant role than ever before.

As we reflect on the impact of DeepSeek's Janus Pro, it becomes clear that this is not just another AI model—it represents a broader shift toward open, collaborative AI ecosystems. The implications of this shift extend far beyond DeepSeek's success, influencing the future of AI research, ethical considerations, and global adoption.

Key Takeaways from Janus Pro's Breakthrough

Janus Pro's success offers several crucial lessons for the AI industry, including insights into technological advancements, market dynamics, and the evolving landscape of AI governance.

1. The Rise of High-Performance, Cost-Effective AI

Historically, cutting-edge AI models have been developed by a few dominant players with massive computational resources. These proprietary models, such as GPT-4 and Google Gemini, have been expensive to train, maintain, and deploy. However, Janus Pro has proven that it is possible to achieve high performance at a fraction of the cost, challenging conventional wisdom about AI scalability.

By demonstrating computational efficiency without sacrificing quality, DeepSeek has set a precedent that:

AI innovation does not require billion-dollar investments—smart optimization techniques can achieve competitive results with fewer resources.

Smaller AI startups and research teams can now compete, thanks to models like Janus Pro reducing the entry barriers.

Open-source AI can drive rapid improvements, as developers worldwide contribute to optimizing and expanding the technology.

This shift toward affordable, high-performance AI means that businesses and researchers no longer need to rely on closed ecosystems to access cutting-edge technology.

2. The Power of Open-Source AI in Driving Industry Growth

Janus Pro's open-source nature has allowed it to gain rapid traction among developers, researchers, and businesses. Unlike proprietary models that require expensive API access and restrictive licensing, Janus Pro offers:

Greater flexibility for developers, allowing customization and integration into specific applications.

A more transparent AI ecosystem, reducing the risks of bias, black-box decision-making, and unethical usage.

A faster innovation cycle, as researchers worldwide can test, modify, and enhance the model without corporate restrictions.

As more companies embrace open AI development, the industry will likely see:

Faster iterations of AI models, with improvements driven by a global community rather than a handful of private companies.

Stronger security and ethical oversight, since open-source models allow for public scrutiny and refinement.

A wider adoption of AI across sectors, as businesses gain access to powerful AI tools without excessive costs.

By making state-of-the-art AI more accessible, Janus Pro has not only democratized AI but also accelerated the pace of AI-driven innovation across multiple industries.

3. Shifting AI Business Models and Market Dynamics

The success of Janus Pro has disrupted traditional AI business models, forcing major companies to rethink their approach to pricing, licensing, and competition. Traditionally, companies like OpenAI and Google have monetized AI through:

Subscription-based API access, where businesses pay per request or usage tier.

Enterprise licensing, where larger organizations pay for AI-powered solutions.

Cloud-based AI services, where AI functionality is embedded within proprietary ecosystems (e.g., Microsoft Azure, Google Cloud).

However, with Janus Pro offering a high-quality, open-source alternative, the market is shifting in several ways:

Companies relying on closed AI models may face pressure to lower costs or offer more transparent pricing structures.

AI businesses will need to focus on value-added services, such as custom AI solutions, training, and integration rather than just selling API access.

Hybrid AI models will emerge, blending open-source flexibility with proprietary enhancements to strike a balance between accessibility and profitability.

This shift means that future AI success will be measured not just by raw model performance, but by how well an AI ecosystem supports innovation, accessibility, and real-world applications.

4. Ethical AI and Regulatory Considerations

As AI technology advances, ethics and governance have become central concerns. The open availability of Janus Pro presents both opportunities and challenges in this area.

Opportunities for Ethical AI Development

Greater transparency in AI research, as open-source models allow researchers to understand, test, and improve AI systems without hidden biases.

Democratization of AI knowledge, preventing a monopoly on AI advancements by a few tech giants.

Better global AI collaboration, as universities, startups, and policymakers can jointly explore ethical AI frameworks.

Potential misuse, as open AI models could be exploited for generating misinformation, deepfakes, or automated cyberattacks.

Regulatory uncertainty, as governments worldwide struggle to define policies that balance innovation with safety.

Accountability concerns, since decentralized AI development means no single entity is fully responsible for an open model's impact.

By taking a proactive approach to AI governance, DeepSeek has an opportunity to set ethical standards for open AI models, ensuring that accessibility does not come at the cost of security or social responsibility.

The release of Janus Pro signals a fundamental shift in how AI is developed, deployed, and monetized. Its impact will be felt across different communities:

For AI Enthusiasts and Researchers

Access to advanced AI without paywalls, enabling experimentation and learning.

Opportunities to contribute to AI improvements, fostering a culture of collaboration and transparency.

More diverse AI applications, as open models allow for creative and unconventional use cases.

For Developers and Startups

Lower costs for AI-driven applications, making it easier to integrate AI into products.

Customization possibilities, allowing businesses to fine-tune AI models for specific needs.

Reduced dependence on large tech companies, increasing competition and innovation.

For Large Enterprises and Governments

A need to adapt business models, as AI accessibility reduces reliance on proprietary solutions.

Growing pressure to define AI regulations, ensuring responsible AI deployment.

More opportunities for public-private AI collaborations, supporting ethical and scalable AI initiatives.

The AI landscape is evolving rapidly, and Janus Pro has positioned itself as a catalyst for change in how AI is developed, shared, and utilized.